YES YES MOUTH

Adham Smart is a writer and translator from London. He was three times a winner of the Foyle Young Poets of the Year Award and has had writing in *The Cadaverine Anthology* (Cadaverine, 2009), *Korsakoff's Paper Chain* (Sidekick Books, 2010) and *The Salt Book of Younger Poets* (Salt, 2011). He has contributed as a translator to the anthology *Six Georgian Poets* (Arc Publications, 2016). *yes yes mouth* is his first solo publication. Find him on Instagram @adhamzaki92.

yes yes mouth

Adham Smart

Valley Press

First published in 2019 by Valley Press
Woodend, The Crescent, Scarborough, YO11 2PW
www.valleypressuk.com

ISBN 978-1-912436-13-2
Cat. no. VP0133

Copyright © Adham Smart 2019

The right of Adham Smart to be identified as the
author of this work has been asserted in accordance with
the Copyright, Designs and Patents Act 1988.

All rights reserved. No part of this publication may be
reproduced, stored in or introduced into a retrieval system,
or transmitted in any form, by any means (electronic,
mechanical, photocopying, recording or otherwise) without
prior written permission from the rights holders.

A CIP record for this book is available from the British Library.

Cover illustration by Beatriz Chivite Ezkieta.
Cover and text design by Jamie McGarry.
Edited by Martha Sprackland.

Contents

And all I do is eat 9
Do you believe in doctors? 10
Sugar is people too 11
İç 12
O, Openmouthed, you are one of us 14
The mock turtle is all things to all men 16
good morning Palestine 17
He tries to paint the egg of the ceramic bird 18
Suck you shelter 19
Arrival 20
As heavy as the bottom of the sea 21
Oh God they're beautiful 22
Bloodsucker 23
How dare you beat them 24
Clinging, clung 26
Mottle 27
How like a rhino is the lumbering priest 28
Blowing glass 29
Aftermath 30
The baby cries in the air 31
Sequence 32
Doppelgangers' dinner party 34
Do all animals dream edible dreams? 35
Why I Google myself 36

*To my family, who have encouraged me since the beginning,
and to my friends, who have written with me since just after.*

And all I do is eat

I go to write and all I do is eat;
my fingers find the food and like the way it feels so much
I sometimes think I'll push it under my nails
so they can have a taste of what leaves their faces greasy.
And when I play tennis I don't play tennis but eat anything everything
clay and Astroturf and your horrible biscuits,
I shovel it all in with my racket hands and they never seem
to hold enough to satisfy my mouth
which is big enough for countries to be founded in.
Or maybe I find a drink of something
and pour it down my throat like a sculptor filling a mould with
gallons and gallons of floury plaster, filling myself
with whatever I can lay my hundred hands on,
music even, I put it on and let it fill my head
like a gardener filling a bucket with slugs and snails
till they're so densely packed the weight begins
to crack shells and suffocate those at the bottom,
I can't get enough, you think I'm not serious but I can't get
serious enough, in my dreams I'm stripping trees from leaf to root
or giving head with the hunger of an animal in the desert,
burying my face so deep I can see the origins of the dark
and softly desperately gulping away like those awful eels called gulper eels,
I'm addicted to my open mouth, I find stuff and I put it in my face,
my mouth when empty is thinking about being filled with anything,
food drink sex worms Tinder smoke kissing paper anything,
anything I see I shove it in my mouth
and I don't care how many teeth I lose. I saw a film
of a farm where geese were piled high
and men stuck a machine called *the hand of god*
in their little long throats and pumped them with grain
till they could barely stand, and this is torture, so why
although there is grain dripping out of my nose and ears
and my hundred hands in bloody twisted knots do I still feel empty
and want you to fill me fill me I'm a sewer
waiting for all the shit in the municipality to come coursing down the drains
into my hungry hungry eager wide wide open yes yes mouth
fill me fill me fill me fill me oh
teach me how to eat myself away and maybe then I'll rest.

Do you believe in doctors?

They laid on hands; there was something regal in their touch.
They knew where to find those lingering tremors, a memory
of sickness, of your whitened face in the dark when the heat
was a hand over your mouth, a stranger at the bottom of the stairs.

In came clerics with their electric choir,
they came to sing you back to health.

I could have read a roll-call of foreign bodies,
and understood what lies your flesh had been told.

Now they lay on hands. Now they peer into the darkness
to sort out right from that which wronged you.
They find an offender, lift it out and jail it,
but like a painting's memory of the brush
there is something in your making
that cannot be erased.

Sugar is people too

The thief is in my mouth again – he knows to pick his marks.
At his footsteps on my tongue I become
a hummingbird-heart of hot-fingered delight,
I want him to visit me nights and rob me senseless.
Even when I'm having sex I'm thinking about
white crystals yawning up through my stomach
and into my chest.

The thief has taken up residence in my mouth.
He has an office and a secretary and prints his name
in sickly serifs on slivers of my teeth. My teeth are the skeletons
of a herd of elephants as small as marbles.

I declare total love on the refined atom thud
of warmth at the bottom of my throat,
its five-finger *You know I'd never leave you*
and I am a puddle of indulgence
and impatience
and incapability
and sweet emptiness.
I am the monster under my own bed.

İç

Why are you here?
I came to take photos.
Why did you stay?
Because I drank lion's milk.
And when you drank it?
My thirst doubled.
And when it doubled?
I fell and kissed the soil.
Was it wet?
It was black and soft.
Was it sweet?
I tasted the bones of the unburied.
Did you bury them?
If they hadn't died I wouldn't be here.
Did you praise them?
I take photos of their burning country.
Why did you cry?
He found me crying and cried with me.
Why did he stop?
He told me their names.
How did you get here?
I cried so much I couldn't speak.
How did you cross the border?
Soldiers love to be photographed with their guns.
What is your name?
He took me to his house and opened a bottle.
What is his name?
He poured out the lion's milk and said 'İç'.
Do you know where you are?
It was transparent but there was no light to shine through it.
Do you know who we are?
The bottle knocked us out and then the planes came.
Why did you come here?
When we woke up no one else did.

Why are you still here?
The children alone took me ten hours.
Who do you fight for?
I came to take photos.
Who do you fight for?
I fight for those who drink lion's milk.
We will kill you.
I only shoot people who are already dead.
We will kill you.
But you will never take the taste off my tongue.

O, Openmouthed, you are one of us

We saw you walking in with frightened steps.
You were blind to candled faces,
shrouded but shining, glowing
at your side. You did not know

the way back and you could not see
what you approached, Child, you did not
understand. We can teach you everything
you do not know. Ah, Child, we saw you shining in,

wings dazzling and eyes declaring 'I am not a burning candle'.
Our hands are clean, our beards are black, our vision
is sharp, yet we are blind, O, we are blind, but surely
we saw you walking in.

Come and lick our bones clean of sin,
read for us the writing on the stone. We read
but do not understand. We are a splintered island
and surely you are glowing, Child. Wash our faces

with your tongue, take us far from this city
where they shroud us in black and push our voices
down below, where we are blind to shining candles
and open wings, where all we have are whispered
emergencies and we blindly fight what we do not
understand, Child, take us in a gasp of burning
air, the kind we all know best, Child, do not
hesitate, we all are waiting, and we can see
you walking weepingly away, but there
is nothing that can frighten you now
for we have conquered your body
and our mark is on your skin
and underneath it in the
places that you do not
know but that we
surely do –

and now be one of us. Ah, Child,
we saw you walking in with frightened steps,
O, Openmouthed, you are one of us!
We saw you walking in.

The mock turtle is all things to all men

I'll be standing at the bar
when you and your friends come in.
You see me, head down,
and I'm too shell to turn you away.
You want to slip me out
and feel me see me naked on the floor
without my own kind
of backbone, but my armour disc collection
doesn't bend like that. I'm different because
that was the only way to be different at the time,
I needed to be more unturtley, less seaweed,
more oats and rye.

I am reptile in my taste in books, mammal in my music,
my scale hands cut bread and my skin ones open cans.
Evolving later doesn't make you better,
it just makes you different, and if my closest relatives
still sometimes walk across each other's tracks
then they must've been equally good
enough to make the cut for this programme we're making
called the modern world.
So I'm standing at the bar
and when you come in I'm going to breathe and
I'm going to think very hard, and you'll
think first and then breathe, and I'll be going home
soon after because I wasn't feeling
that kind of night.

good morning Palestine

this is your captain speaking
five-hundred metres
from your window

look at us
the red and grey
we fly at you

ugly birds
all talon and tusk

the fire we harbour
in frosty canisters
with messages
in children's chalk

the smell
of burning textbooks

a shroud of dust
on his tiny face

He tries to paint the egg of the ceramic bird

He painted books of dolloped inks curled into feathers, beaks done in thick-cut yellow and black, eggs so delicate blue they made the yolks blush. Into his sweaty memory and back out again flew those large pages, washed in colour, pages warm as new milk, birds in every corner and on every axis, wingtip to wingtip in a circle dance, colours like nothing he would see again except in moments of rage when they roared up in fiery plumes behind his eyes.

The greedy years swallowed each other, and now here he was, fuggy tent-man in a throbbing bouquet of a jungle, red eyes and pale lips, pencil slipping through his slick fingers. Brown feathers. Unremarkable call. Average wingspan. Tiny eggs. The smallest, the hardest, the smoothest, the most handsome egg of all the egg-laying creatures in the world, so shellingly perfect they called it ceramic, and sent a painter to distil its essence onto cream paper.

When he first laid his eyes on one of these bright beads of birdlife he yelled with joy and howled with grief, and he knew that there would be no more concentratedly beautiful egg for him to first lay eyes on again, and that he was finished; not even with a hundred hands and twelve oceans of paint in different shades of white could he hope to trap in pigment the pure goodness of this egg. And all his midnight training and all his squinted experience and all his love of birds and paints were smoke and sawdust. Its marble smallness would never be more than a ghost in the muscles of his wrist.

And now he is a sad waxy man in a canvas nest, building and destroying entire worlds of eggs. And all around him the beaked canopy, the chattering hooligan forest, is quiet. They watch him from above, unblinking they watch him fail, fail, fail.

Suck you shelter

Sneak me in – do you feel the heat
yes – apocalypse me in my clothes
compass-pin me to the room four corners
shelter me in your sunset temple
my lips around your second knuckle
sex me here a hundred hands
hell for leather, suck you bed
shelter you fire, burn you lips
fiery lakes we drank to be wicked
your gasps fit like a glove
if you ever breathe I'll disappear
crumble me into powder
spread me on your lips
shelter me in night places
your body-like-a-glove
mouth me wicked
sneak in me
hear me sex
the burning bed
heaven can't breathe
suck hundred hands
take me galaxies
fit me in you
we fit in sunset
apocalypse mouth
the lava and the magma
we melt and
flood

Arrival

I learn from you to speak like underwater.
And the murmurs and the curling black.
And me and him thinking through the swash.
In the middle of your meaning
wrap up the stories in billowing words.
Oil-speaking soft on the ears,
pooled language – history in a circle,
circles in circles, everything again and again,
the unending unpacking of sounds and sights
into me and you and they want to speak to us.
Horoscope speech, wrapped around.
And in the words thrumming
through the shell of cloud.
At the feet of the smoke-column
swimming words
every memory:
reunpack and push through the fog.

Are you learning?

Can you read me?

Let's start with the pronouns.

As heavy as the bottom of the sea

They woke to find an angel on the beach
as heavy as the bottom of the sea,
as dark as boulders locked in frozen lakes:
a swallower of oceans run aground.

A fleet of barnacles, a host of worms
and gulls and crabs with long legs took their toll.
The ribs, caved in, immense and cracked and bruised,
the bloated tongue pitted by tiny mouths.

The tail that thrashed, the water-weary jaws,
the crumpled architecture of the back,
the twilight throat – all whispers of a whale
that sank before their eyes into the sand.

Oh God they're beautiful

but then how ugly you feel
to think that they're beautiful. And then waves
of times you were ugly bear down like big dogs,
and your mind is a beach and they are
beautiful tourists who come here
all the time but don't bother to learn
how to say *thank you* in the language
or bother to Google why
the fishermen throw back all the little ones.
They're so beautiful
they've left none for you, it's not your fault
you're ugly! But in the archives
you find that actually
beauty's never been more abundant,
it's twelve cents a barrel, China have so much
they're storing it in silos, and yet even though
the world's up to the teeth with it
you are uglier
than the bubbling remains
of a howler monkey
torn apart by our closest
biological relatives. Children
in bed
in every time zone
wake up
with Guernica faces
their voices
peeling the paint
because you are known
to be so ugly.

Bloodsucker

Two leeches lying on a fluff-muddy riverbed look at each other with their big round mouths. They're both thinking the same thing: if I bit that one's tail and they bit mine, we'd end up as a circle of blood going round and round and that would be the whole story forever. Well, those two put their idea into practice, and left us in the mess we're in today: a crisis-level leech shortage in a country overflowing with leech-rings, rolling around like drunk cyclists or comedy hubcaps, encircling and drawing attention to the small things that people drop. All the other animals, myself included, are bitter to the teeth that they can't just latch onto another being and that way sustain themselves forever.

How dare you beat them

The pagan language
you beat it out of them
your tongue is not so holy
how dare you beat them

Pagan leaves by the riverbank
the children speak to them
the plants unfurl their names
how dare you beat them

The serpent made the speaking rivers
your dreams sing wrong of them
the serpent speaks the children's language
how dare you beat them

You make the children bleed and cry
you grunt and force your strength on them
you force your language into their mouths
you beat the language out of them

The children know not what they say
you grunt forgiveness and hit their bones
they scream as you beat it out of them
at night the darkness drips on them
they smother their language in its sleep
how dare you beat them

The devil never spoke to them
he speaks to you in your land
demons mutter under your skin
your blood speaks to them
you bleed the devil from children's backs
how dare you beat them

Belt stick whip wall
you nightly talk to them
they speak in shadows
your words taste of nothing
how dare you beat them

Your hands are not kind
your teachers hated them
you hate the children's dark eyes
how dare you beat them

The children sing the serpent words
you shout and persecute them
they fly kites and whistle at you
the land turns its face from you
how dare you beat them

You beat them to make them remember
the holy language you teach them
you beat them to make them forget
the language heaving inside them

Black and brown
red you beat them
you do God's work
how dare you beat them

Clinging, clung

When I saw you crossing the bridge
and the river hobbling away
and the floaters in the fetid water
and the stained mouths of the white birds
as they pecked and picked and spat
and sometimes sank,
I wondered about your drinking.
Lids and wrappers and smoking guns,
inverted mountains of filth
fatberging through the sea,
the cast of hangers-on
fed and fouled by their landfill lord
who no-one can plead with,
there is no intercession,
the false god of the ocean,
bad evolution of land and water,
at once cloud and fist, at glance mist but in fact
death riding the surf
to the summit in the open seas
where blue and red and green and purple
pour cups of themselves into animals
and lap up the sickness.
Maybe you will do politics
when you find it in the toilet bowl when you piss.

Mottle

A froglet floats in a lazy pond, little fingers splayed,
loamy dreams behind his eyes.
His throat quivers like a drumskin,
his nostrils are droplets of tea on an envelope.

His existence began in a writhing jelly
and will end small and crushed among the wet leaves.
For now his stillness is a wafer of scum, a tuft of moss,
and as the sun spills into the camouflaged kingdom
he is a soft-skinned prince waking up.

How like a rhino is the lumbering priest

How like a rhino is the lumbering priest, wrapped in He-terminology,
like an old man left to die too far from the fire, or
a forsaken tortoise, fattened then scooped from its shell. His
rhino-skin, sugarlumps in tar, defiles his skullcap.
Is he not ugly? Is he not a monster, like a gargoyle in the snow?
The question may be one of faith, and in this regard he is beautiful;
lumbering priest, giving wine and bread, ringing the bells. This crumpled
priest, however, is ugly still, and no less so for his being
wrapped in the confessions of the small people. His dry blessing –
in nomine patris, et cetera – tolls with dusty sleep, deep in women's hearts.
He knows the Greek for 'love', the Hebrew for 'grace', but
terminology will not save him from the loneliness of his face.

Blowing glass

A big man stands up – he's going to blow some glass.
He's going to gulp down draughts of air and fill
a ball of glass with billowing swells.
He closes his eyes.

that sweet transfer of weight
into the bud ballooning at your feet
Before every tidal wave the sea catches its breath
the water is reeled in
a mile back and we see how
the sand goes on and on beneath
and then comes the world of water with a gaping mouth.

Now, when he takes the blowpipe
and puts his lips to the copper,
although his padlock chest is
already surging with the stuff
he draws in a wisp of air
from the core of the heavy,
boiling bead. In that
pinhead moment
of ebb and flow, man and glass
trade memories of being sand.

Aftermath

And on the day the sun rose in the west,
the wide-eyed ones were mustered in their masses
to tell the world to stay inside and look
no further than the line of tape, no longer
than it takes to fill the bath, look nowhere other
than down. Look or don't look, we won't stop you;
cold hands and cracked lips will make you turn
your head away. Avoid, avoid it all
like picking up the phone in lightning weather.
Don't come to us with swooping banners,
there is no time. Curse us to the seventh generation
in every blood-born language if it helps, but
you will not go outside. It's not forbidden,
it's simply not an option any more.
Your house is now the only breathing home,
and that's the same for everyone. Drag your
bodies itching to the windows, open them
and smell the ashy wind, remember how
you like your food in cans, and while you wonder
how scrambled eggs without the eggs will taste,
we will remind you of the burnt-out days
we have survived to be here now.
Stormish banners sweeping the streets
and bodies thickening under earthworm skies,
cities in ash, the hooting mouths of non-survivors,
bile in fossil burbles caulking up from cokey lungs,
seven years of thousandfold destruction
unmake the land. Look, friends,
we are protecting you from this.

The baby cries in the air

I watched the baby rise;
it was a cake, and it cried
butter and rainbows
running down its face
because it was rising
because mum picked it up
and it wanted to crawl
maybe learn how to walk
or stay soft and cluggy
and not rise and become firm
and full of air
but be dense and heavy forever
and never know the lightness
of rising, of being
about to be eaten.

Sequence

Translation from Georgian of Rati Amaghlobeli's Sekvencia

A and B and C and D
I don't understand what's happened to me,
I want a sister, I'll hold her hand, Amen
and B and C and D and
I want to escape this skin, I want to be free and
restart my life from the one-two-three and
run from death, I'll somehow manage,
somehow withstand, and I'll shoulder up to Golgotha
my Fate-dealt cards, my rotten hand
of rains and stormy destiny. *A*
and B and C and D and
I tried but I couldn't expand
on sadness' vast geometry and
fortune's thirteen latitudes,
I call out from its deepest C and—
A, B, C, D
and slowly surely *E, F* and
G, H, and I, I want a *J, K,*
la-la-la-lullaby, flay the panther's skin
from this body-be-damned, I'm going to Jerusalem,
I want to drink at the wedding at Cana,
I want shepherds to walk with, a brother-band.
M and N, O and P and
Q, R, S and T and
the fruits of my garden husbandry
brought in from fields in Canaan's sand.
I recognised U in the skies and
V and W and X and
I want to escape this moment, I want to see
two horizons celestially spanned.
I don't want the straight and narrow,
give me roads, I want ten thousand;

a road that leads from the moon and stars,
another that leads me to you,
I want the sound of the sun's opening belly and
Y and Z and A and B and
Aries' forehead, Taurus too, I want that road
to the spheres, I want to brand
every planet with its own hot secrets.
I want to go to every star,
I want to burn in every star,
I want to transform every star,
I want to escape this moment, I want
skies, firmaments blue and grand.
A, B, C and D and
O God, brighten my forehead's forecast
light up like nine suns, Amen, and
now A-want, E-want
white I-want, O-want
I'll flee from wars, from land to land
until I reach this life's *Ω-want*—
one great *U-want*,
one raw paradise apple and
then next to you, if you want.
A, B, C, and,
God, understand – I want a sister.

Doppelgangers' dinner party

Open wide, you guzzling men!
Your throats are rippling with sweet beer.
You eat and drink and eat again,
you snort dreams cut in lines and smear
sickness on the back of your gums.

You electric eels, you sit and gorge
on drunk pears and exploded plums.
In your biggest thickest hands you forge
dragon signatures, spitting guns,
kisses that taste like pencil lead.

You engage the meat – you suck the bones
and swallow gobbets slick and red,
you smash big fruit into telephones
and wonder why the line is dead,
then look up, licking your mad eyes.

You filthy dribblers, you toothless boys,
you turn off the lights and talk in sighs.
While the world is up to its neck in noise
and dogs suit up and evangelise,
you get an amorous feeling between your toes.

Doppelgangers fuck doppelgangers.
Your rusty love comes to a close
when partisans and weapon-clangers
come shooting up the churning rows
of doppelgangers banging in the dark.

We're waiting for you in the square.
In low voices we remark
how choked your mouths are and your hair.
The game's up, gangers. The street dogs bark;
you've nowhere to hide. We've nothing to fear.

Do all animals dream edible dreams?

I am the tree, knotholed and aging,
you are the beetle, preying on air.

Spiracles, wing-cases, spiracles, wings;
you are made of one hundred ingredients.

Your feathery eyes are furred with pollen,
my branches are oozing with green.

The blood that flows between us
is light as airborne seeds
and I can reach, with my tree-teeth,
and eat up all your dreams.

Why I Google myself

- To remember how to spell my name
- Myspace still there?
- Faster than calling my mum and asking
- Muscle memory got me doing myself again
- Numerology on the number of unique hits; calculate the day on which to hold my wedding
- Find out if there's some way I can add myself as a friend on Facebook
- If I Google myself enough will they pay me royalties?
- Fantasise about being Adham Shaikh
- See if I can catch other people Googling me
- Remind myself what I've done (maybe I'll do it again?)
- If I Google myself enough will they ask me to be a consultant?
- Pour scorn on Adham Faramawy
- How to get red wine stains out of white wine shirts
- Species of wasp coincidentally also called Adham Smart
- So that when people Google something beginning with 'A' or 'S' in my browser they'll see how many times I've looked and with how many variations
- Unexpected tips on garden safety
- Observe any changes in results and either a) sigh because inertia or b) weep because can't handle change
- Try to use Ask Jeeves but then realise I'm probably better off asking Adham Smart
- What if one day nothing? What if all the Adhams in their Shaikh and Faramawy and other guises conspire to squeeze me out of the written world, replicate in the cells of my online presence and burst my name apart, and then all I am is a boy in a room in a city, with habits but no habitat, connected but unplugged, drinking endless glasses of water and looking up from the empty screen at the ceiling where I've stuck pieces of paper saying   DON'T | WASTE | YOUR | TIME

Lightning Source UK Ltd.
Milton Keynes UK
UKHW010109300519
343551UK00001B/34/P